PENNSYLVANIA RULES
2018 Edition

Updated through January 1, 2018

Michigan Legal Publishing Ltd.
QUICK DESK REFERENCE SERIES™

Academic and bulk discounts available at
www.michlp.com

WE WELCOME YOUR FEEDBACK: info@michlp.com

ISBN-13: 978-1-64002-036-8

Contents

Article I. General Provisions..1
  Rule 101. Scope; Adoption and Citation....................................1
  Rule 102. Purpose 1
  Rule 103. Rulings on Evidence 1
  Rule 104. Preliminary Questions 2
  Rule 105. Limiting Evidence That is Not Admissible Against Other
  Parties or for Other Purposes 2
  Rule 106. Remainder of or Related Writings or Recorded Statements 2

Article II. Judicial Notice 3
  Rule 201. Judicial Notice of Adjudicative Facts 3

Article III. Presumptions...5
  Rule 301. Presumptions 5

Article IV. Relevance and its Limits 7
  Rule 401. Test for Relevant Evidence...7
  Rule 402. General Admissibility of Relevant Evidence...........7
  Rule 403. Excluding Relevant Evidence for Prejudice, Confusion, Waste
  of Time, or Other Reasons 7
  Rule 404. Character Evidence; Crimes or Other Acts..............7
  Rule 405. Methods of Proving Character....................................8
  Rule 406. Habit; Routine Practice..9
  Rule 407. Subsequent Remedial Measures 9
  Rule 408. Compromise Offers and Negotiations 9
  Rule 409. Offers to Pay Medical and Similar Expenses 10
  Rule 410. Pleas, Plea Discussions, and Related Statements 10
  Rule 411. Liability Insurance 11
  Rule 412. Sex Offense Cases: The Victim's Sexual Behavior or
  Predisposition (Not Adopted) 11

Article V. Privileges 13
  Rule 501. Privileges 13

Article VI. Witnesses 15
  Rule 601. Competency 15
  Rule 602. Need for Personal Knowledge 15
  Rule 603. Oath or Affirmation to Testify Truthfully 15
  Rule 604. Interpreter 15
  Rule 605. Judge's Competency as a Witness............................15
  Rule 606. Juror's Competency as a Witness 15
  Rule 607. Who May Impeach a Witness, Evidence to Impeach a Witness
 16
  Rule 608. A Witness's Character for Truthfulness or Untruthfulness ...16
  Rule 609. Impeachment by Evidence of a Criminal Conviction............17

Rule 610. Religious Beliefs or Opinions 17
Rule 611. Mode and Order of Examining Witnesses and Presenting
Evidence 17
Rule 612. Writing or Other Item Used to Refresh a Witness's Memory 18
Rule 613. Witness's Prior Inconsistent Statement to Impeach; Witness's
Prior Consistent Statement to Rehabilitate 19
Rule 614. Court's Calling or Examining a Witness 19
Rule 615. Sequestering Witnesses 20

Article VII. Opinions and Expert Testimony 21
Rule 701. Opinion Testimony by Lay Witnesses 21
Rule 702. Testimony by Expert Witnesses 21
Rule 703. Bases of an Expert's Opinion Testimony 21
Rule 704. Opinion on an Ultimate Issue 21
Rule 705. Disclosing the Facts or Data Underlying an Expert's Opinion
.... 21
Rule 706. Court-Appointed Expert Witnesses 21

Article VIII. Hearsay 23
Rule 801. Definitions that Apply to this Article 23
Rule 802. The Rule Against Hearsay 23
Rule 803. Exceptions to the Rule Against Hearsay-Regardless of
Whether the Declarant Is Available as a Witness 23
Rule 803.1. Exceptions to the Rule Against Hearsay-Testimony of
Declarant Necessary 26
Rule 804. Exceptions to the Rule Against Hearsay- When the Declarant
is Unavailable as a Witness 27
Rule 805. Hearsay Within Hearsay 29
Rule 806. Attacking and Supporting the Declarant's Credibility 29

Article IX. Authentication and Identification 31
Rule 901. Authenticating or Identifying Evidence 31
Rule 902. Evidence That is Self-Authenticating 32
Rule 903. Subscribing Witness's Testimony 34

Article X. Contents of Writings, Recordings, and Photographs 35
Rule 1001. Definitions That Apply to This Article 35
Rule 1002. Requirement of the Original 35
Rule 1003. Admissibility of Duplicates 35
Rule 1004. Admissibility of Other Evidence of Content 35
Rule 1005. Copies of Public Records to Prove Content 36
Rule 1006. Summaries to Prove Content 36
Rule 1007. Testimony or Statement of a Party to Prove Content 36
Rule 1008. Functions of the Court and Jury 36

Article I. General Provisions

Rule 101. Scope; Adoption and Citation

(a) **Scope**. These rules of evidence govern proceedings in all courts of the Commonwealth of Pennsylvania's unified judicial system, except as otherwise provided by law.

(b) **Adoption and Citation**. These rules of evidence are adopted by the Supreme Court of Pennsylvania under the authority of Article V § 10(c) of the Constitution of Pennsylvania, adopted April 23, 1968. They shall be known as the Pennsylvania Rules of Evidence and shall be cited as "Pa.R.E."

Rule 102. Purpose

These rules should be construed so as to administer every proceeding fairly, eliminate unjustifiable expense and delay, and promote the development of evidence law, to the end of ascertaining the truth and securing a just determination.

Rule 103. Rulings on Evidence

(a) **Preserving a Claim of Error**. A party may claim error in a ruling to admit or exclude evidence only:
   (1) if the ruling admits evidence, a party, on the record:
      (A) makes a timely objection, motion to strike, or motion in limine; and
      (B) states the specific ground, unless it was apparent from the context; or
   (2) if the ruling excludes evidence, a party informs the court of its substance by an offer of proof, unless the substance was apparent from the context.

(b) **Not Needing to Renew an Objection or Offer of Proof**. Once the court rules definitively on the record-either before or at trial-a party need not renew an objection or offer of proof to preserve a claim of error for appeal.

(c) **Court's Statement About the Ruling; Directing an Offer of Proof**. The court may make any statement about the character or form of the evidence, the objection made, and the ruling. The court may direct that an offer of proof be made in question-and-answer form.

(d) **Preventing the Jury from Hearing Inadmissible Evidence**. To the extent practicable, the court must conduct a jury trial so that inadmissible evidence is not suggested to the jury by any means.

Rule 104. Preliminary Questions

(a) **In General**. The court must decide any preliminary question about whether a witness is qualified, a privilege exists, or evidence is admissible. In so deciding, the court is not bound by evidence rules, except those on privilege.

(b) **Relevance That Depends on a Fact**. When the relevance of evidence depends on whether a fact exists, proof must be introduced sufficient to support a finding that the fact does exist. The court may admit the proposed evidence on the condition that the proof be introduced later.

(c) **Conducting a Hearing So That the Jury Cannot Hear it**. The court must conduct any hearing on a preliminary question so that the jury cannot hear it if:

    (1) the hearing involves evidence alleged to have been obtained in violation of the defendant's rights;

    (2) a defendant in a criminal case is a witness and so requests; or

    (3) justice so requires.

(d) **Cross-Examining a Defendant in a Criminal Case**. By testifying on a preliminary question, a defendant in a criminal case does not become subject to cross-examination on other issues in the case.

(e) **Weight and Credibility**. Even though the court rules that evidence is admissible, this does not preclude a party from offering other evidence relevant to the weight or credibility of that evidence.

Rule 105. Limiting Evidence That is Not Admissible Against Other Parties or for Other Purposes

If the court admits evidence that is admissible against a party or for a purpose-but not against another party or for another purpose-the court, on timely request, must restrict the evidence to its proper scope and instruct the jury accordingly. The court may also do so on its own initiative.

Rule 106. Remainder of or Related Writings or Recorded Statements

If a party introduces all or part of a writing or recorded statement, an adverse party may require the introduction, at that time, of any other part-or any other writing or recorded statement-that in fairness ought to be considered at the same time.

Article II. Judicial Notice

Rule 201. Judicial Notice of Adjudicative Facts

(a) **Scope**. This rule governs judicial notice of an adjudicative fact only, not a legislative fact.

(b) **Kinds of Facts That May Be Judicially Noticed**. The court may judicially notice a fact that is not subject to reasonable dispute because it:

    (1) is generally known within the trial court's territorial jurisdiction; or

    (2) can be accurately and readily determined from sources whose accuracy cannot reasonably be questioned.

(c) **Taking Notice**. The court:

    (1) may take judicial notice on its own; or

    (2) must take judicial notice if a party requests it and the court is supplied with the necessary information.

(d) **Timing**. The court may take judicial notice at any stage of the proceeding.

(e) **Opportunity to Be Heard**. On timely request, a party is entitled to be heard on the propriety of taking judicial notice and the nature of the fact to be noticed. If the court takes judicial notice before notifying a party, the party, on request, is still entitled to be heard.

(f) **Instructing the Jury**. The court must instruct the jury that it may, but is not required to, accept as conclusive any fact judicially noticed.

Article III. Presumptions

Rule 301. Presumptions

Presumptions as they now exist or may be modified by law shall be unaffected by the adoption of these rules.

Rule 301. Presumptions

Article IV. Relevance and its Limits

Rule 401. Test for Relevant Evidence

Evidence is relevant if:
(a) it has any tendency to make a fact more or less probable than it would be without the evidence; and
(b) the fact is of consequence in determining the action.

Rule 402. General Admissibility of Relevant Evidence

All relevant evidence is admissible, except as otherwise provided by law. Evidence that is not relevant is not admissible.

Rule 403. Excluding Relevant Evidence for Prejudice, Confusion, Waste of Time, or Other Reasons

The court may exclude relevant evidence if its probative value is outweighed by a danger of one or more of the following: unfair prejudice, confusing the issues, misleading the jury, undue delay, wasting time, or needlessly presenting cumulative evidence.

Rule 404. Character Evidence; Crimes or Other Acts

(a) **Character Evidence**.
  (1) *Prohibited Uses.* Evidence of a person's character or character trait is not admissible to prove that on a particular occasion the person acted in accordance with the character or trait.
  (2) *Exceptions for a Defendant or Victim in a Criminal Case.* The following exceptions apply in a criminal case:
     (A) a defendant may offer evidence of the defendant's pertinent trait, and if the evidence is admitted, the prosecutor may offer evidence to rebut it;
     (B) subject to limitations imposed by statute a defendant may offer evidence of an alleged victim's pertinent trait, and if the evidence is admitted the prosecutor may:
        (i) offer evidence to rebut it; and
        (ii) offer evidence of the defendant's same trait; and
     (C) in a homicide case, the prosecutor may offer evidence of the alleged victim's trait of peacefulness to rebut evidence that the victim was the first aggressor.
  (3) *Exceptions for a Witness.* Evidence of a witness's character may be admitted under Rules 607, 608, and 609.

(4) *Exception in a Civil Action for Assault and Battery*. In a civil action for assault and battery, evidence of the plaintiff's character trait for violence may be admitted when offered by the defendant to rebut evidence that the defendant was the first aggressor.

(b) **Crimes, Wrongs or Other Acts**.

(1) *Prohibited Uses*. Evidence of a crime, wrong, or other act is not admissible to prove a person's character in order to show that on a particular occasion the person acted in accordance with the character.

(2) *Permitted Uses*. This evidence may be admissible for another purpose, such as proving motive, opportunity, intent, preparation, plan, knowledge, identity, absence of mistake, or lack of accident. In a criminal case this evidence is admissible only if the probative value of the evidence outweighs its potential for unfair prejudice.

(3) *Notice in a Criminal Case*. In a criminal case the prosecutor must provide reasonable notice in advance of trial, or during trial if the court excuses pretrial notice on good cause shown, of the general nature of any such evidence the prosecutor intends to introduce at trial.

Rule 405. Methods of Proving Character

(a) **By Reputation**. When evidence of a person's character or character trait is admissible, it may be proved by testimony about the person's reputation. Testimony about the witness's opinion as to the character or character trait of the person is not admissible.

(1) On cross-examination of the character witness, the court may allow an inquiry into relevant specific instances of the person's conduct probative of the character trait in question.

(2) In a criminal case, on cross-examination of a character witness, inquiry into allegations of other criminal conduct by the defendant, not resulting in conviction, is not permissible.

(b) **By Specific Instances of Conduct**. Specific instances of conduct are not admissible to prove character or a trait of character, except:

(1) In a civil case, when a person's character or a character trait is an essential element of a claim or defense, character may be proved by specific instances of conduct.

(2) In a criminal case, when character or a character trait of an alleged victim is admissible under Pa.R.E. 404(a)(2)(B) the defendant may prove the character or character trait by specific instances of conduct.

Rule 406. Habit; Routine Practice

Evidence of a person's habit or an organization's routine practice may be admitted to prove that on a particular occasion the person or organization acted in accordance with the habit or routine practice. The court may admit this evidence regardless of whether it is corroborated or there was an eyewitness.

Rule 407. Subsequent Remedial Measures

When measures are taken by a party that would have made an earlier injury or harm less likely to occur, evidence of the subsequent measures is not admissible against that party to prove:
- negligence;
- culpable conduct;
- a defect in a product or its design; or
- a need for a warning or instruction.

But the court may admit this evidence for another purpose such as impeachment or-if disputed-proving ownership, control, or the feasibility of precautionary measures.

Rule 408. Compromise Offers and Negotiations

(a) **Prohibited Uses**. Evidence of the following is not admissible-on behalf of any party-either to prove or disprove the validity or amount of a disputed claim or to impeach by a prior inconsistent statement or a contradiction:

    (1) furnishing, promising, or offering-or accepting, promising to accept, or offering to accept-a valuable consideration in compromising or attempting to compromise the claim; and

    (2) conduct or a statement made during compromise negotiations about the claim.

(b) **Exceptions**. The court may admit this evidence for another purpose, such as proving a witness's bias or prejudice, negating a contention of undue delay, or proving an effort to obstruct a criminal investigation or prosecution.

Pa. R.E. 408 is consistent with 42 Pa.C.S. § 6141 which provides, in pertinent part, as follows:

§ 6141. Effect of certain settlements

(a) **Personal Injuries**. Settlement with or any payment made to an injured person or to others on behalf of such injured person with the permission of such injured person or to anyone entitled to recover damages on account of injury or death of such person shall not constitute an admission of liability by the person making the payment or on whose behalf the payment was made, unless the parties to such settlement or payment agree to the contrary.

(b) **Damages to Property**. Settlement with or any payment made to a person or on his behalf to others for damages to or destruction of property shall not constitute an admission of liability by the person making the payment or on whose behalf the payment was made, unless the parties to such settlement or payment agree to the contrary.

(c) **Admissibility in Evidence**. Except in an action in which final settlement and release has been pleaded as a complete defense, any settlement or payment referred to in subsections (a) and (b) shall not be admissible in evidence on the trial of any matter.

Rule 409. Offers to Pay Medical and Similar Expenses

Evidence of furnishing, promising to pay, or offering to pay medical, hospital, or similar expenses resulting from an injury is not admissible to prove liability for the injury.

Rule 410. Pleas, Plea Discussions, and Related Statements

(a) **Prohibited Uses**. In a civil or criminal case, evidence of the following is not admissible against the defendant who made the plea or participated in the plea discussions:

(1) a guilty plea that was later withdrawn;

(2) a nolo contendere plea;

(3) a statement made in the course of any proceedings under Rules 311, 313, 409, 414, 424, 550 or 590 of the Pennsylvania Rules of Criminal Procedure, Rule 11 of the Federal Rules of Criminal Procedure, or a comparable rule or procedure of another state; or

(4) a statement made during plea discussions with an attorney for the prosecuting authority if the discussions did not result in a guilty plea or they resulted in a later withdrawn guilty plea.

(b) **Exceptions**. The court may admit a statement described in Rule 410(a)(3) or (4):

(1) in any proceeding in which another statement made during the same plea or plea discussions has been introduced, if in fairness the statements ought to be considered together; or

(2) in a criminal proceeding for perjury, false swearing or unsworn falsification to authorities, if the defendant made the statement under oath, on the record, and with counsel present.

There is also a statute governing the admissibility of guilty pleas and pleas of nolo contendere in cases charging summary motor vehicle violations when offered in civil cases arising out of the same facts. See 42 Pa.C.S. § 6142 which provides:

(a) **General Rule**. A plea of guilty or nolo contendere, or a payment of the fine and costs prescribed after any such plea, in any summary proceeding made by any person charged with a violation of Title 75 (relating to vehicles) shall not be admissible as evidence in any civil matter arising out of the same violation or under the same facts or circumstances.

(b) **Exception**. The provisions of subsection (a) shall not be applicable to administrative or judicial proceedings involving the suspension of a motor vehicle or tractor operating privilege, learner's permit, or right to apply for a motor vehicle or tractor operating privilege, or the suspension of a certificate of appointment as an official inspection station, or the suspension of a motor vehicle, tractor, or trailer registration.

Rule 411. Liability Insurance

Evidence that a person was or was not insured against liability is not admissible to prove whether the person acted negligently or otherwise wrongfully. But the court may admit this evidence for another purpose, such as proving a witness's bias or prejudice or proving agency, ownership, or control.

Rule 412. Sex Offense Cases: The Victim's Sexual Behavior or Predisposition (Not Adopted)

18 Pa.C.S. § 3104 provides:

§ 3104. Evidence of victim's sexual conduct
(a) **General rule**. Evidence of specific instances of the alleged victim's past sexual conduct, opinion evidence of the alleged victim's past sexual conduct, and reputation evidence of the alleged victim's past sexual conduct shall not be admissible in prosecutions under this chapter except evidence of the alleged victim's past sexual conduct with the defendant where consent of the alleged victim is at issue and such evidence is otherwise admissible pursuant to the rules of evidence.
(b) **Evidentiary proceedings**. A defendant who proposes to offer evidence of the alleged victim's past sexual conduct pursuant to subsection (a) shall file a written motion and offer of proof at the time

of trial. If, at the time of trial, the court determines that the motion and offer of proof are sufficient on their faces, the court shall order an in camera hearing and shall make findings on the record as to the relevance and admissibility of the proposed evidence pursuant to the standards set forth in subsection (a).

Article V. Privileges

Rule 501. Privileges

Privileges as they now exist or may be modified by law shall be unaffected by the adoption of these rules.

Rule 501. Privileges

Article VI. Witnesses

Rule 601. Competency

(a) **General Rule**. Every person is competent to be a witness except as otherwise provided by statute or in these rules.

(b) **Disqualification for Specific Defects**. A person is incompetent to testify if the court finds that because of a mental condition or immaturity the person:

    (1) is, or was, at any relevant time, incapable of perceiving accurately;

    (2) is unable to express himself or herself so as to be understood either directly or through an interpreter;

    (3) has an impaired memory; or

    (4) does not sufficiently understand the duty to tell the truth.

Rule 602. Need for Personal Knowledge

A witness may testify to a matter only if evidence is introduced sufficient to support a finding that the witness has personal knowledge of the matter. Evidence to prove personal knowledge may consist of the witness's own testimony. This rule does not apply to a witness's expert testimony under Rule 703.

Rule 603. Oath or Affirmation to Testify Truthfully

Before testifying, a witness must give an oath or affirmation to testify truthfully. It must be in a form designed to impress that duty on the witness's conscience.

Rule 604. Interpreter

An interpreter must be qualified and must give an oath or affirmation to make a true translation.

Rule 605. Judge's Competency as a Witness

The presiding judge may not testify as a witness at the trial or other proceeding.

Rule 606. Juror's Competency as a Witness

(a) **At the Trial**. A juror may not testify as a witness before the other jurors at the trial. If a juror is called to testify, the court must give a party an opportunity to object outside the jury's presence.

(b) During an Inquiry into the Validity of a Verdict

(1) *Prohibited Testimony or Other Evidence.* During an inquiry into the validity of a verdict, a juror may not testify about any statement made or incident that occurred during the jury's deliberations; the effect of anything on that juror's or another juror's vote; or any juror's mental processes concerning the verdict. The court may not receive a juror's affidavit or evidence of a juror's statement on these matters.

(2) *Exceptions.* A juror may testify about whether:

(A) prejudicial information not of record and beyond common knowledge and experience was improperly brought to the jury's attention; or

(B) an outside influence was improperly brought to bear on any juror.

Rule 607. Who May Impeach a Witness, Evidence to Impeach a Witness

(a) **Who May Impeach a Witness**. Any party, including the party that called the witness, may attack the witness's credibility.

(b) **Evidence to Impeach a Witness**. The credibility of a witness may be impeached by any evidence relevant to that issue, except as otherwise provided by statute or these rules.

Rule 608. A Witness's Character for Truthfulness or Untruthfulness

(a) **Reputation Evidence**. A witness's credibility may be attacked or supported by testimony about the witness's reputation for having a character for truthfulness or untruthfulness. But evidence of truthful character is admissible only after the witness's character for truthfulness has been attacked. Opinion testimony about the witness's character for truthfulness or untruthfulness is not admissible.

(b) **Specific Instances of Conduct**. Except as provided in Rule 609 (relating to evidence of conviction of crime),

(1) the character of a witness for truthfulness may not be attacked or supported by cross-examination or extrinsic evidence concerning specific instances of the witness' conduct; however,

(2) in the discretion of the court, the credibility of a witness who testifies as to the reputation of another witness for truthfulness or untruthfulness may be attacked by cross-examination concerning specific instances of conduct (not including arrests) of the other witness, if they are probative of truthfulness or untruthfulness; but extrinsic evidence thereof is not admissible.

Rule 609. Impeachment by Evidence of a Criminal Conviction

(a) **In General**. For the purpose of attacking the credibility of any witness, evidence that the witness has been convicted of a crime, whether by verdict or by plea of guilty or nolo contendere, must be admitted if it involved dishonesty or false statement.

(b) **Limit on Using the Evidence After 10 Years**. This subdivision (b) applies if more than 10 years have passed since the witness's conviction or release from confinement for it, whichever is later. Evidence of the conviction is admissible only if:

    (1) its probative value substantially outweighs its prejudicial effect; and

    (2) the proponent gives an adverse party reasonable written notice of the intent to use it so that the party has a fair opportunity to contest its use.

(c) **Effect of Pardon or Other Equivalent Procedure**. Evidence of a conviction is not admissible under this rule if the conviction has been the subject of one of the following:

    (1) a pardon or other equivalent procedure based on a specific finding of innocence; or

    (2) a pardon or other equivalent procedure based on a specific finding of rehabilitation of the person convicted, and that person has not been convicted of any subsequent crime.

(d) **Juvenile Adjudications**. In a criminal case only, evidence of the adjudication of delinquency for an offense under the Juvenile Act, 42 Pa.C.S. §§ 6301 et seq., may be used to impeach the credibility of a witness if conviction of the offense would be admissible to attack the credibility of an adult.

(e) **Pendency of an Appeal**. A conviction that satisfies this rule is admissible even if an appeal is pending. Evidence of the pendency is also admissible.

Rule 610. Religious Beliefs or Opinions

Evidence of a witness's religious beliefs or opinions is not admissible to attack or support the witness's credibility.

Rule 611. Mode and Order of Examining Witnesses and Presenting Evidence

(a) **Control by the Court; Purposes**. The court should exercise reasonable control over the mode and order of examining witnesses and presenting evidence so as to:

    (1) make those procedures effective for determining the truth;

    (2) avoid wasting time; and

    (3) protect witnesses from harassment or undue embarrassment.

(b) **Scope of Cross-Examination**. Cross-examination of a witness other than a party in a civil case should be limited to the subject matter of the direct examination and matters affecting credibility, however, the court may, in the exercise of discretion, permit inquiry into additional matters as if on direct examination. A party witness in a civil case may be cross-examined by an adverse party on any matter relevant to any issue in the case, including credibility, unless the court, in the interests of justice, limits the cross-examination with respect to matters not testified to on direct examination.

(c) **Leading Questions**. Leading questions should not be used on direct or redirect examination except as necessary to develop the witness's testimony. Ordinarily, the court should allow leading questions:

    (1) on cross-examination; and

    (2) when a party calls a hostile witness, an adverse party, or a witness identified with an adverse party. A witness so examined should usually be interrogated by all other parties as to whom the witness is not hostile or adverse as if under redirect examination.

Rule 612. Writing or Other Item Used to Refresh a Witness's Memory

(a) **Right to Refresh Memory**. A witness may use a writing or other item to refresh memory for the purpose of testifying while testifying, or before testifying.

(b) **Rights of Adverse Party**.

    (1) If a witness uses a writing or other item to refresh memory while testifying, an adverse party is entitled to have it produced at the hearing, trial or deposition, to inspect it, to cross-examine the witness about it, and to introduce in evidence any portion that relates to the witness's testimony.

    (2) If a witness uses a writing or other item to refresh memory before testifying, and the court in its discretion determines it is necessary in the interests of justice, an adverse party is entitled to have it produced at the hearing, trial or deposition, to inspect it, to cross-examine the witness about it, and to introduce in evidence any portion that relates to the witness's testimony.

(c) **Rights of Producing Party**. If the producing party claims that the writing or other item includes unrelated matter, the court must examine it in camera, delete any unrelated portion, and order that the rest be delivered to the adverse party. Any portion deleted over objection must be preserved for the record.

(d) **Failure to Produce or Deliver**. If the writing or other item is not produced or is not delivered as ordered, the court may issue any appropriate order. But if the prosecution does not comply in a criminal case, the court must strike the witness's testimony or-if justice so requires-declare a mistrial, or the court may use contempt procedures.

Rule 613. Witness's Prior Inconsistent Statement to Impeach; Witness's Prior Consistent Statement to Rehabilitate

(a) **Witness's Prior Inconsistent Statement to Impeach**. A witness may be examined concerning a prior inconsistent statement made by the witness to impeach the witness's credibility. The statement need not be shown or its contents disclosed to the witness at that time, but on request, the statement or contents must be shown or disclosed to an adverse party's attorney.

(b) **Extrinsic Evidence of a Witness's Prior Inconsistent Statement**. Unless the interests of justice otherwise require, extrinsic evidence of a witness's prior inconsistent statement is admissible only if, during the examination of the witness,

(1) the statement, if written, is shown to, or if not written, its contents are disclosed to, the witness;

(2) the witness is given an opportunity to explain or deny the making of the statement; and

(3) an adverse party is given an opportunity to question the witness.

This paragraph does not apply to an opposing party's statement as defined in Rule 803(25).

(c) **Witness's Prior Consistent Statement to Rehabilitate**. Evidence of a witness's prior consistent statement is admissible to rehabilitate the witness's credibility if the opposing party is given an opportunity to cross-examine the witness about the statement and the statement is offered to rebut an express or implied charge of:

(1) fabrication, bias, improper influence or motive, or faulty memory and the statement was made before that which has been charged existed or arose; or

(2) having made a prior inconsistent statement, which the witness has denied or explained, and the consistent statement supports the witness's denial or explanation.

Rule 614. Court's Calling or Examining a Witness

(a) **Calling**. Consistent with its function as an impartial arbiter, the court, with notice to the parties, may call a witness on its own or at a party's request. Each party is entitled to cross-examine the witness.

(b) **Examining**. Where the interest of justice so requires, the court may examine a witness regardless of who calls the witness.

(c) **Objections**. A party may object to the court's calling or examining a witness when given notice that the witness will be called or when the witness is examined. When requested to do so, the court must give the objecting party an opportunity to make objections out of the presence of the jury.

Rule 615. Sequestering Witnesses

At a party's request the court may order witnesses sequestered so that they cannot learn of other witnesses' testimony. Or the court may do so on its own. But this rule does not authorize sequestering:

(a) a party who is a natural person;

(b) an officer or employee of a party that is not a natural person (including the Commonwealth) after being designated as the party's representative by its attorney;

(c) a person whose presence a party shows to be essential to presenting the party's claim or defense; or

(d) a person authorized by statute or rule to be present.

Article VII. Opinions and Expert Testimony

Rule 701. Opinion Testimony by Lay Witnesses

If a witness is not testifying as an expert, testimony in the form of an opinion is limited to one that is:
(a) rationally based on the witness's perception;
(b) helpful to clearly understanding the witness's testimony or to determining a fact in issue; and
(c) not based on scientific, technical, or other specialized knowledge within the scope of Rule 702.

Rule 702. Testimony by Expert Witnesses

A witness who is qualified as an expert by knowledge, skill, experience, training, or education may testify in the form of an opinion or otherwise if:
(a) the expert's scientific, technical, or other specialized knowledge is beyond that possessed by the average layperson;
(b) the expert's scientific, technical, or other specialized knowledge will help the trier of fact to understand the evidence or to determine a fact in issue; and
(c) the expert's methodology is generally accepted in the relevant field.

Rule 703. Bases of an Expert's Opinion Testimony

An expert may base an opinion on facts or data in the case that the expert has been made aware of or personally observed. If experts in the particular field would reasonably rely on those kinds of facts or data in forming an opinion on the subject, they need not be admissible for the opinion to be admitted.

Rule 704. Opinion on an Ultimate Issue

An opinion is not objectionable just because it embraces an ultimate issue.

Rule 705. Disclosing the Facts or Data Underlying an Expert's Opinion

If an expert states an opinion the expert must state the facts or data on which the opinion is based.

Rule 706. Court-Appointed Expert Witnesses

Where the court has appointed an expert witness, the witness appointed must advise the parties of the witness's findings, if any. The witness may be called to testify by the court or any party. The witness shall be subject to cross-examination by any party, including a party calling the witness. In civil cases, the witness's deposition may be taken by any party.

Article VIII. Hearsay

Rule 801. Definitions that Apply to this Article

(a) **Statement**. "Statement" means a person's oral assertion, written assertion, or nonverbal conduct, if the person intended it as an assertion.
(b) **Declarant**. "Declarant" means the person who made the statement.
(c) **Hearsay**. "Hearsay" means a statement that
    (1) the declarant does not make while testifying at the current trial or hearing; and
    (2) a party offers in evidence to prove the truth of the matter asserted in the statement.

Rule 802. The Rule Against Hearsay

Hearsay is not admissible except as provided by these rules, by other rules prescribed by the Pennsylvania Supreme Court, or by statute.

Rule 803. Exceptions to the Rule Against Hearsay-Regardless of Whether the Declarant Is Available as a Witness

The following are not excluded by the rule against hearsay, regardless of whether the declarant is available as a witness:
    (1) **Present Sense Impression**. A statement describing or explaining an event or condition, made while or immediately after the declarant perceived it.
    (2) **Excited Utterance**. A statement relating to a startling event or condition, made while the declarant was under the stress of excitement that it caused.
    (3) **Then-Existing Mental, Emotional, or Physical Condition**. A statement of the declarant's then-existing state of mind (such as motive, intent or plan) or emotional, sensory, or physical condition (such as mental feeling, pain, or bodily health), but not including a statement of memory or belief to prove the fact remembered or believed unless it relates to the validity or terms of the declarant's will.
    (4) **Statement Made for Medical Diagnosis or Treatment**. A statement that:
        (A) is made for-and is reasonably pertinent to-medical treatment or diagnosis in contemplation of treatment; and
        (B) describes medical history, past or present symptoms, pain, or sensations, or the inception or general character of the cause

or external source thereof, insofar as reasonably pertinent to treatment, or diagnosis in contemplation of treatment.

(5) **Recorded Recollection** (Not Adopted)

(6) **Records of a Regularly Conducted Activity**. A record (which includes a memorandum, report, or data compilation in any form) of an act, event or condition if:

    (A) the record was made at or near the time by-or from information transmitted by-someone with knowledge;

    (B) the record was kept in the course of a regularly conducted activity of a ''business'', which term includes business, institution, association, profession, occupation, and calling of every kind, whether or not conducted for profit;

    (C) making the record was a regular practice of that activity;

    (D) all these conditions are shown by the testimony of the custodian or another qualified witness, or by a certification that complies with Rule 902(11) or (12) or with a statute permitting certification; and

    (E) the opponent does not show that the source of information or other circumstances indicate a lack of trustworthiness.

(7) **Absence of a Record of a Regularly Conducted Activity** (Not Adopted)

(8) **Public Records**. A record of a public office if:

    (A) the record describes the facts of the action taken or matter observed;

    (B) the recording of this action or matter observed was an official public duty; and

    (C) the opponent does not show that the source of the information or other circumstances indicate a lack of trustworthiness.

(9) **Public Records of Vital Statistics** (Not Adopted)

(10) **Non-Existence of a Public Record**. Testimony-or a certification-that a diligent search failed to disclose a public record if:

    (A) the testimony or certification is admitted to prove that

        (i) the record does not exist; or

        (ii) a matter did not occur or exist, if a public office regularly kept a record for a matter of that kind.

    (B) in a criminal case:

        (i) the attorney for the Commonwealth who intends to offer a certification files and serves written notice of that intent upon the defendant's attorney or, if unrepresented, the defendant, at least 20 days before trial; and

        (ii) defendant's attorney or, if unrepresented, the defendant, does not file and serve a written demand for testimony in lieu of the certification within 10 days of service of the notice.

(11) **Records of Religious Organizations Concerning Personal or Family History**. A statement of birth, legitimacy, ancestry, marriage, divorce, death, relationship by blood or marriage, or similar facts of personal or family history, contained in a regularly kept record of a religious organization.

(12) **Certificates of Marriage, Baptism, and Similar Ceremonies**. A statement of fact contained in a certificate:

    (A) made by a person who is authorized by a religious organization or by law to perform the act certified;

    (B) attesting that the person performed a marriage or similar ceremony or administered a sacrament; and

    (C) purporting to have been issued at the time of the act or within a reasonable time after it.

(13) **Family Records**. A statement of fact about personal or family history contained in a family record, such as a Bible, genealogy, chart, engraving on a ring, inscription on a portrait, or engraving on an urn or burial marker.

(14) **Records of Documents That Affect an Interest in Property**. The record of a document that purports to establish or affect an interest in property if:

    (A) the record is admitted to prove the content of the original recorded document, along with its signing and its delivery by each person who purports to have signed it;

    (B) the record is kept in a public office; and

    (C) a statute authorizes recording documents of that kind in that office.

(15) **Statements in Documents That Affect an Interest in Property**. A statement contained in a document, other than a will, that purports to establish or affect an interest in property if the matter stated was relevant to the document's purpose-unless later dealings with the property are inconsistent with the truth of the statement or the purport of the document.

(16) **Statements in Ancient Documents**. A statement in a document that is at least 30 years old and whose authenticity is established.

(17) **Market Reports and Similar Commercial Publications**. Market quotations, lists, directories, or other compilations that are generally relied on by the public or by persons in particular occupations.

(18) **Statements in Learned Treatises, Periodicals, or Pamphlets** (Not Adopted)

(19) **Reputation Concerning Personal or Family History**. A reputation among a person's family by blood, adoption, or marriage-or among a person's associates or in the community-concerning the person's birth, adoption, legitimacy, ancestry, marriage, divorce, death, relationship by blood, adoption, or marriage, or similar facts of personal or family history.

(20) **Reputation Concerning Boundaries or General History**. A reputation in a community-arising before the controversy-concerning boundaries of land in the community or customs that affect the land, or concerning general historical events important to that community, state or nation.

(21) **Reputation Concerning Character**. A reputation among a person's associates or in the community concerning the person's character.

(22) **Judgment of a Previous Conviction** (Not Adopted)

(23) **Judgments Involving Personal, Family, or General History or a Boundary** (Not Adopted)

(24) **Other Exceptions** (Not Adopted)

(25) **An Opposing Party's Statement**. The statement is offered against an opposing party and:

    (A) was made by the party in an individual or representative capacity;

    (B) is one the party manifested that it adopted or believed to be true;

    (C) was made by a person whom the party authorized to make a statement on the subject;

    (D) was made by the party's agent or employee on a matter within the scope of that relationship and while it existed; or

    (E) was made by the party's coconspirator during and in furtherance of the conspiracy.

The statement may be considered but does not by itself establish the declarant's authority under (C); the existence or scope of the relationship under (D); or the existence of the conspiracy or participation in it under (E).

Rule 803.1. Exceptions to the Rule Against Hearsay-Testimony of Declarant Necessary

The following statements are not excluded by the rule against hearsay if the declarant testifies and is subject to cross-examination about the prior statement:

(1) **Prior Inconsistent Statement of Declarant-Witness**. A prior statement by a declarant-witness that is inconsistent with the declarant-witness's testimony and:
   (A) was given under oath subject to the penalty of perjury at a trial, hearing, or other proceeding, or in a deposition;
   (B) is a writing signed and adopted by the declarant; or
   (C) is a verbatim contemporaneous electronic recording of an oral statement.

(2) **Prior Statement of Identification by Declarant-Witness**. A prior statement by a declarant-witness identifying a person or thing, made after perceiving the person or thing, provided that the declarant-witness testifies to the making of the prior statement.

(3) **Recorded Recollection of Declarant-Witness**. A memorandum or record made or adopted by a declarant-witness that:
   (A) is on a matter the declarant-witness once knew about but now cannot recall well enough to testify fully and accurately;
   (B) was made or adopted by the declarant-witness when the matter was fresh in his or her memory; and
   (C) the declarant-witness testifies accurately reflects his or her knowledge at the time when made.

   If admitted, the memorandum or record may be read into evidence and received as an exhibit, but may be shown to the jury only in exceptional circumstances or when offered by an adverse party.

(4) **Prior Statement by a Declarant-Witness Who Claims an Inability to Remember the Subject Matter of the Statement**. A prior statement by a declarant-witness who testifies to an inability to remember the subject matter of the statement, unless the court finds the claimed inability to remember to be credible, and the statement:
   (A) was given under oath subject to the penalty of perjury at a trial, hearing, or other proceeding, or in a deposition;
   (B) is a writing signed and adopted by the declarant; or
   (C) is a verbatim contemporaneous electronic recording of an oral statement.

Rule 804. Exceptions to the Rule Against Hearsay- When the Declarant is Unavailable as a Witness

(a) **Criteria for Being Unavailable**. A declarant is considered to be unavailable as a witness if the declarant:
   (1) is exempted from testifying about the subject matter of the declarant's statement because the court rules that a privilege applies;

(2) refuses to testify about the subject matter despite a court order to do so;

(3) testifies to not remembering the subject matter, except as provided in Rule 803.1(4) ;

(4) cannot be present or testify at the trial or hearing because of death or a then-existing infirmity, physical illness, or mental illness; or

(5) is absent from the trial or hearing and the statement's proponent has not been able, by process or other reasonable means, to procure:

   (A) the declarant's attendance, in the case of a hearsay exception under Rule 804(b)(1) or (6) ; or

   (B) the declarant's attendance or testimony, in the case of a hearsay exception under Rule 804(b)(2), (3), or (4).

But this paragraph (a) does not apply if the statement's proponent procured or wrongfully caused the declarant's unavailability as a witness in order to prevent the declarant from attending or testifying.

(b) **The Exceptions**. The following are not excluded by the rule against hearsay if the declarant is unavailable as a witness:

   (1) *Former Testimony*. Testimony that:

      (A) was given as a witness at a trial, hearing, or lawful deposition, whether given during the current proceeding or a different one; and

      (B) is now offered against a party who had-or, in a civil case, whose predecessor in interest had-an opportunity and similar motive to develop it by direct, cross-, or redirect examination.

   (2) *Statement Under Belief of Imminent Death*. A statement that the declarant, while believing the declarant's death to be imminent, made about its cause or circumstances.

   (3) *Statement Against Interest*. A statement that:

      (A) a reasonable person in the declarant's position would have made only if the person believed it to be true because, when made, it was so contrary to the declarant's proprietary or pecuniary interest or had so great a tendency to invalidate the declarant's claim against someone else or to expose the declarant to civil or criminal liability; and

      (B) is supported by corroborating circumstances that clearly indicate its trustworthiness, if it is offered in a criminal case as one that tends to expose the declarant to criminal liability.

   (4) *Statement of Personal or Family History*. A statement made before the controversy arose about:

      (A) the declarant's own birth, adoption, legitimacy, ancestry, marriage, divorce, relationship by blood, adoption or marriage, or similar facts of personal or family history, even though the declarant had no way of acquiring personal knowledge about that fact; or

(B) another person concerning any of these facts, as well as death, if the declarant was related to the person by blood, adoption, or marriage or was so intimately associated with the person's family that the declarant's information is likely to be accurate.

(5) *Other exceptions* (Not Adopted)

(6) *Statement Offered Against a Party That Wrongfully Caused the Declarant's Unavailability*. A statement offered against a party that wrongfully caused-or acquiesced in wrongfully causing-the declarant's unavailability as a witness, and did so intending that result.

Rule 805. Hearsay Within Hearsay

Hearsay within hearsay is not excluded by the rule against hearsay if each part of the combined statements conforms with an exception to the rule.

Rule 806. Attacking and Supporting the Declarant's Credibility

When a hearsay statement has been admitted in evidence, the declarant's credibility may be attacked, and then supported, by any evidence that would be admissible for those purposes if the declarant had testified as a witness. The court may admit evidence of the declarant's inconsistent statement or conduct, regardless of when it occurred or whether the declarant had an opportunity to explain or deny it. If the party against whom the statement was admitted calls the declarant as a witness, the party may examine the declarant on the statement as if on cross-examination.

Article IX. Authentication and Identification

Rule 901. Authenticating or Identifying Evidence

(a) **In General**. To satisfy the requirement of authenticating or identifying an item of evidence, the proponent must produce evidence sufficient to support a finding that the item is what the proponent claims it is.

(b) **Examples**. The following are examples only-not a complete list-of evidence that satisfies the requirement:

    (1) *Testimony of a Witness with Knowledge*. Testimony that an item is what it is claimed to be.

    (2) *Nonexpert Opinion about Handwriting*. A nonexpert's opinion that handwriting is genuine, based on a familiarity with it that was not acquired for the current litigation.

    (3) *Comparison by an Expert Witness or the Trier of Fact*. A comparison with an authenticated specimen by an expert witness or the trier of fact.

    (4) *Distinctive Characteristics and the Like*. The appearance, contents, substance, internal patterns, or other distinctive characteristics of the item, taken together with all the circumstances.

    (5) *Opinion About a Voice*. An opinion identifying a person's voice-whether heard firsthand or through mechanical or electronic transmission or recording-based on hearing the voice at any time under circumstances that connect it with the alleged speaker.

    (6) *Evidence About a Telephone Conversation*. For a telephone conversation, evidence that a call was made to the number assigned at the time to:

        (A) a particular person, if circumstances, including self-identification, show that the person answering was the one called; or

        (B) a particular business, if the call was made to a business and the call related to business reasonably transacted over the telephone.

    (7) *Evidence About Public Records*. Evidence that:

        (A) a document was recorded or filed in a public office as authorized by law; or

        (B) a purported public record or statement is from the office where items of this kind are kept.

    (8) *Evidence About Ancient Documents or Data Compilations*. For a document or data compilation, evidence that it:

        (A) is in a condition that creates no suspicion about its authenticity;

        (B) was in a place where, if authentic, it would likely be; and

(C) is at least 30 years old when offered.

(9) *Evidence About a Process or System.* Evidence describing a process or system and showing that it produces an accurate result.

(10)*Methods Provided by a Statute or a Rule.* Any method of authentication or identification allowed by a statute or a rule prescribed by the Supreme Court.

Rule 902. Evidence That is Self-Authenticating

The following items of evidence are self-authenticating; they require no extrinsic evidence of authenticity in order to be admitted:

(1) **Domestic Public Documents That are Sealed and Signed**. A document that bears:
   (A) a seal purporting to be that of the United States; any state, district, commonwealth, territory, or insular possession of the United States; the former Panama Canal Zone; the Trust Territory of the Pacific Islands; a political subdivision of any of these entities; or a department, agency, or officer of any entity named above; and
   (B) a signature purporting to be an execution or attestation.

(2) **Domestic Public Documents that are not Sealed but are Signed and Certified**. A document that bears no seal if:
   (A) it bears the signature of an officer or employee of an entity named in Rule 902(1)(A); and
   (B) another public officer who has a seal and official duties within that same entity certifies under seal-or its equivalent-that the signer has the official capacity and that the signature is genuine.

(3) **Foreign Public Documents**. A document that purports to be signed or attested by a person who is authorized by a foreign country's law to do so. The document must be accompanied by a final certification that certifies the genuineness of the signature and official position of the signer or attester-or of any foreign official whose certificate of genuineness relates to the signature or attestation or is in a chain of certificates of genuineness relating to the signature or attestation. The certification may be made by a secretary of a United States embassy or legation; by a consul general, vice consul, or consular agent of the United States; or by a diplomatic or consular official of the foreign country assigned or accredited to the United States. If all parties have been given a reasonable opportunity to investigate the document's authenticity and accuracy, the court may for good cause, either:
   (A) order that it be treated as presumptively authentic without final certification; or

    (B) allow it to be evidenced by an attested summary with or without final certification.

(4) **Certified Copies of Public Records**. A copy of an official record-or a copy of a document that was recorded or filed in a public office as authorized by law-if the copy is certified as correct by:

    (A) the custodian or another person authorized to make the certification; or

    (B) a certificate that complies with Rule 902(1), (2), or (3), a statute or a rule prescribed by the Supreme Court.

(5) **Official Publications**. A book, pamphlet, or other publication purporting to be issued by a public authority.

(6) **Newspapers and Periodicals**. Printed material purporting to be a newspaper or periodical.

(7) **Trade Inscriptions and the Like**. An inscription, sign, tag, or label purporting to have been affixed in the course of business and indicating origin, ownership, or control.

(8) **Acknowledged Documents**. A document accompanied by a certificate of acknowledgment that is lawfully executed by a notary public or another officer who is authorized to take acknowledgments.

(9) **Commercial Paper and Related Documents**. Commercial paper, a signature on it, and related documents, to the extent allowed by general commercial law.

(10) **Presumptions Authorized by Statute**. A signature, document, or anything else that a statute declares to be presumptively or prima facie genuine or authentic.

(11) **Certified Domestic Records of a Regularly Conducted Activity**. The original or a copy of a domestic record that meets the requirements of Rule 803(6)(A)-(C), as shown by a certification of the custodian or another qualified person that complies with Pa.R.C.P. No. 76. Before the trial or hearing, the proponent must give an adverse party reasonable written notice of the intent to offer the record-and must make the record and certification available for inspection-so that the party has a fair opportunity to challenge them.

(12) **Certified Foreign Records of a Regularly Conducted Activity**. In a civil case, the original or a copy of a foreign record that meets the requirements of Rule 902(11), modified as follows: the certification rather than complying with a statute or Supreme Court rule, must be signed in a manner that, if falsely made, would subject the maker to a criminal penalty in the country

where the certification is signed. The proponent must also meet the notice requirements of Rule 902(11).

(13) **Certificate of Non-Existence of a Public Record**. A certificate that a document was not recorded or filed in a public office as authorized by law if certified by the custodian or another person authorized to make the certificate.

Rule 903. Subscribing Witness's Testimony

A subscribing witness's testimony is necessary to authenticate a writing only if required by the law of the jurisdiction that governs its validity.

Article X. Contents of Writings, Recordings, and Photographs

Rule 1001. Definitions That Apply to This Article

In this article:

(a) A "writing" consists of letters, words, numbers, or their equivalent set down in any form.

(b) A "recording" consists of letters, words, numbers, or their equivalent recorded in any manner.

(c) A "photograph" means a photographic image or its equivalent stored in any form.

(d) An "original" of a writing or recording means the writing or recording itself or any counterpart intended to have the same effect by the person who executed or issued it. For electronically stored information, "original" means any printout-or other output readable by sight-if it accurately reflects the information. An "original" of a photograph includes the negative or a print from it.

(e) A "duplicate" means a copy produced by a mechanical, photographic, chemical, electronic, or other equivalent process or technique that accurately reproduces the original.

Rule 1002. Requirement of the Original

An original writing, recording, or photograph is required in order to prove its content unless these rules, other rules prescribed by the Supreme Court, or a statute provides otherwise.

Rule 1003. Admissibility of Duplicates

A duplicate is admissible to the same extent as the original unless a genuine question is raised about the original's authenticity or the circumstances make it unfair to admit the duplicate.

Rule 1004. Admissibility of Other Evidence of Content

An original is not required and other evidence of the content of a writing, recording, or photograph is admissible if:

(a) all the originals are lost or destroyed, and not by the proponent acting in bad faith;

(b) an original cannot be obtained by any available judicial process;

(c) the party against whom the original would be offered had control of the original; was at that time put on notice, by pleadings or otherwise, that the original would be a subject of proof at the trial or hearing; and fails to produce it at the trial or hearing; or

(d) the writing, recording, or photograph is not closely related to a controlling issue.

Rule 1005. Copies of Public Records to Prove Content

The proponent may use a copy to prove the content of an official record-or of a document that was recorded or filed in a public office as authorized by law-if these conditions are met: the record or document is otherwise admissible; and the copy is certified as correct in accordance with Rule 902(4) or is testified to be correct by a witness who has compared it with the original. If no such copy can be obtained by reasonable diligence, then the proponent may use other evidence to prove the content.

Rule 1006. Summaries to Prove Content

The proponent may use a summary, chart, or calculation to prove the content of voluminous writings, recordings, or photographs that cannot be conveniently examined in court. The proponent must make the originals or duplicates available for examination or copying, or both, by other parties at a reasonable time and place. And the court may order the proponent to produce them in court.

Rule 1007. Testimony or Statement of a Party to Prove Content

The proponent may prove the content of a writing, recording, or photograph by the testimony, deposition, or written statement of the party against whom the evidence is offered. The proponent need not account for the original.

Rule 1008. Functions of the Court and Jury

Ordinarily, the court determines whether the proponent has fulfilled the factual conditions for admitting other evidence of the content of a writing, recording, or photograph under Rule 1004 or 1005. But in a jury trial, the jury determines-in accordance with Rule 104(b)-any issue about whether:

(a) an asserted writing, recording, or photograph ever existed;

(b) another one produced at the trial or hearing is the original; or

(c) other evidence of content accurately reflects the content.

www.ingramcontent.com/pod-product-compliance
Lightning Source LLC
Chambersburg PA
CBHW060514220326
41598CB00025B/3659